Maria Luisa Banfi

A Faraway World

Illustrated by
LibellulArt

Teen ELi Readers

Teen Eli Readers

The **ELI Readers** collection is a complete range of books and plays for readers of all ages, ranging from captivating contemporary stories to timeless classics. There are four series, each catering for a different age group: **First ELI Readers, Young ELI Readers, Teen ELI Readers** and **Young Adult ELI Readers**. The books are carefully edited and beautifully illustrated to capture the essence of the stories and plots. The readers are supplemented with 'Focus on' texts packed with background cultural information about the writers and their lives and times.

A Faraway World
By Maria Luisa Banfi
Language Level Consultant
Silvana Sardi
Illustrated by **LibellulArt**
Activities by **Angela Tomkinson**

ELI Readers
Founder and Series Editors
Paola Accattoli, Grazia Ancillani, Daniele Garbuglia (Art Director)

Graphic Design
Andersen the Premedia Company

Production Manager
Francesco Capitano

Photo credits
Shutterstock, Marka

New edition: **2021**
First edition: **2009**

P.O. Box 6
62019 Recanati (MC)
Italy
T +39 071750701
F +39 071977851
info@elionline.com
www.elionline.com

Typeset in 12 / 17 pt
Fulmar designed by Leo Philp

Printed in Italy by
Tecnostampa - Pigini Group Printing Division
Loreto - Trevi (Italia) - ERT201.10
ISBN 978-88-536-3193-0

Contents

Main Characters

Marquat *14 years old, he lives in Cardiff with his parents. He doesn't like it when people say he's from Africa. Cardiff is his home.*

Alex
He's Marquat's only friend, but he isn't good at school like him.

A classmate
He doesn't like Marquat and laughs at his name.

Jay & Kylie
Two girls in Marquat's class at school. They try to talk to him, but he's very shy.

Marquat's father
He's got a supermarket and works hard. Money is very important for him.

Marquat's mother
She tells Marquat that school is important but he must also help at home.

Marquat's sisters
They're younger than Marquat and he has to take them to school in the morning and do other.
things for them.

Bullies
The bullies are horrible to Marquat because his family is from Africa.

Before you read

Vocabulary

1 Read the sentences describing things about school and complete the words.

The exercises you do at home after school: h o m e w o r k

1 The school you go to after nursery school: p _ _ _ _ _ _ school

2 French, physics, music, drama are all examples: s _ _ _ _ _ _ _

3 In the classroom you usually sit at a d _ _ _ .

4 It's where you eat your lunch at school: c _ _ _ _ _ _

5 The person who works in a school and teaches the students: t _ _ _ _ _ _

2 Match the parts of the body with the pictures.

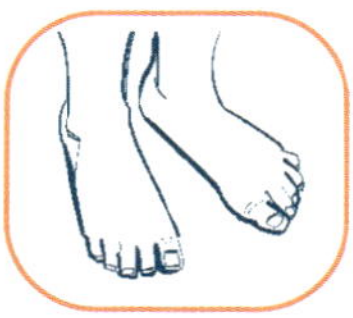

1 feet

2 ______

3 ______

4 ______

5 ______

6 ______

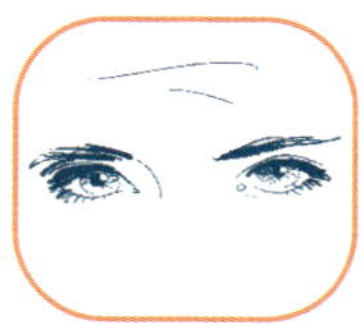

7 ______

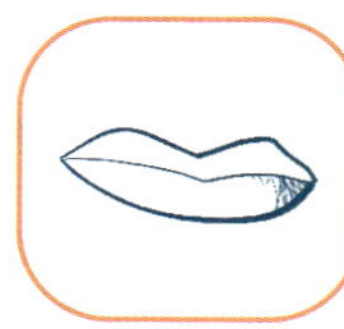

8 ______

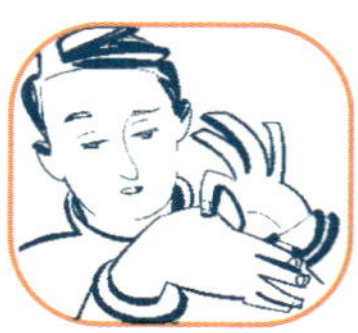

9 ______

10 ______

a lips	**b** mouth	**c** skin	**d** eyes	**e** face
f hand	**g** body	~~**h**~~ feet	**i** back	**j** nose

Speaking

3 This story is about a boy called Marquat who lives in Wales, but his grandparents live in Nigeria. Answer these questions with a partner. Use the Internet to help you.

21st Century Skills

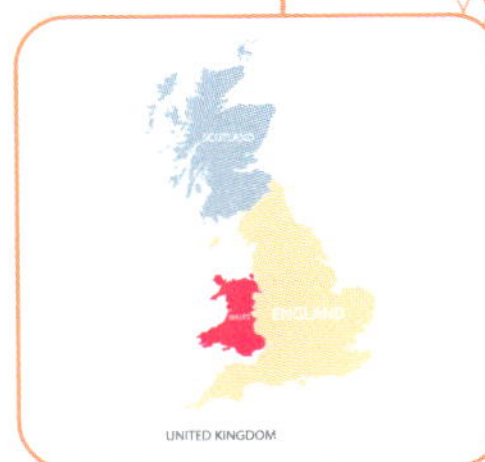

1. Where's Nigeria and what's its capital?
2. How many countries are there in Africa?
3. Where's Wales and what's its capital?
4. How many countries are there in Great Britain?
5. How many people live in Nigeria?
6. How many people live in Wales?
7. Which of these two countries would you prefer to visit? Why?

Listening

2 **4 Listen to the start of Chapter 1 and write one word in each space.**

Marquat

Age: *14 years old*

He lives in a small (1) ________ .

His parents come from (2) ________

Today, Marquat is going to a new (3) ________

School starts at (4) ________

Marquat has two little (5) ________ .

Chapter 1

The New School

▶ 2 MARQUAT is 14 years old. He lives with his family in Cardiff, Wales. They live in a small flat in Westgate Street, near Bute Park. His parents come from Nigeria, a country in Africa, but Marquat feels British because his home is here, in Britain.

Marquat's parents are from Nigeria but he feels British because he lives in Wales. This is his first day at a new school.

Today is a very important day for him because it's his first day at the new school: new classmates, new teachers, new everything!

School starts at about 9.15, but before going to school Marquat has to take his two little sisters to their schools: one is at nursery school[1] and the other is at primary school[2].

[1] **nursery school** the school you go to between 3 and 5 years of age
[2] **primary school** the school you go to between 5 and 10 years of age

A Faraway World

Marquat's mother always says to him, 'School is important, Marquat, but you have to help at home, too!' Marquat knows this and he usually helps his mother at home.

When he's got time, he also works in his father's supermarket. Marquat doesn't like working in the supermarket because he finds it really boring! He prefers reading and studying, but his father doesn't understand this, 'Marquat, you study too much! Why don't you work for me and make some money? I know school is important, but money is, too!'

Marquat helps his mother at home and also works in his father's supermarket. His father thinks he studies too much.

His mum and dad always talk about money. They work very hard and they make enough money to look after the family and the house.

Marquat's parents work hard and send money to Marquat's grandparents in Nigeria.

They also send money back to Nigeria where Marquat's grandparents still live. Marquat's mother always says that they need money. 'Poor Grandma and Grandpa!' thinks Marquat to himself.

Marquat is good at school and he wants to go to university and then to be a journalist. He always sits at the front of the class near the teacher.

Marquat wants to study. When he finishes school, he wants to go to Cardiff University and then he wants to find a job as a journalist[1].
It's very hard when you have to study and work at the same time, but he knows he can do it!

Marquat learns things very fast - faster than his classmates. All his teachers know this and one of them, his English teacher, always says, 'You have to keep[2] studying, Marquat, because you've got a bright future ahead of you[3]!'

›

Here is Marquat with his family. He's ready to take his sisters to school before he goes to his new school.

[1] **journalist** a person who writes for a newspaper
[2] **keep doing something** not stop doing something
[3] **a bright future ahead of you** your future looks very good

THE UNITED IRISHMAN

Marquat tries to be friendly to the boy sitting next to him, but everyone in the class laughs when they hear Marquat's name. The next day Marquat has nobody sitting next to him.

In class, Marquat sits at the front. There's always a free desk there. His new classmates don't usually like sitting at the front because they're too close to the teacher! They like sitting at the back.

The boy sitting next to Marquat is small and wears glasses.

Marquat smiles at him and says, 'Hi, I'm …' but he doesn't finish his sentence because the boy puts a finger to his lips[1] and says, 'Shhh …'

Just then[2], the teacher walks in and explains what they're going to study this year. Then he calls out[3] everybody's name.

When he says, 'Marquat!' all the other students look at him because his name

[1] **put a finger to (your) lips** move (your) finger to (your) mouth to say 'be quiet'
[2] **just then** at that moment
[3] **call out** read, say

isn't English. The small boy sitting next to him asks, 'What's your name?' but he doesn't wait for Marquat to answer. He just laughs.

The next day, when Marquat goes and sits at his desk, he's all alone.

At school, most of his classmates don't talk to Marquat and they call him a swot because he studies hard. Only two girls try to speak to him, but Marquat is too shy to answer. He thinks nobody likes him.

Marquat's classmates don't talk to him very much. At school, Marquat knows everything. He always answers the teacher's questions and he always does his homework.

'He's a swot[1]!' says the small boy with the glasses. He doesn't like Marquat.

Kylie and Jay are two girls in his class. They sometimes talk to Marquat, but he's very shy[2] and quiet. He just answers 'yes' or 'no' when they ask him something.

1 **swot** (slang) a person who works very hard at school
2 **shy** if you're shy, you find it difficult to talk to other people

Marquat's mum doesn't understand why he thinks the colour of his skin stops him having friends. She's got lots of friends.

He doesn't talk to anyone because he thinks that nobody likes him.

'My skin's black,' he says to his mum, 'and I'm very good at school. That's why nobody likes me.'

His mother looks at him, confused[1], 'Marquat, that's ridiculous[2]! I've got black skin, too, but I've got lots of friends. A lot of people have got black skin. That doesn't mean you can't have friends! You're very special, my love[3], especially[4] because you're so good at school!' she smiles.

Think

Do you talk to your parents like Marquat when you're sad about something?

[1] **confused** (here) she doesn't understand
[2] **ridiculous** silly
[3] **my love** (here) a kind way of talking to somebody
[4] **especially** above all

The boy with the glasses doesn't like Marquat because he's good at school.

BLK
LPS

Reading A2 Key

1 Choose the correct answer for each question about Chapter 1.

Where does Marquat live?

~~A~~ Wales **B** Nigeria **C** England

1 Where does Marquat have to take his sisters?

A Home **B** To school **C** To the supermarket

2 Who does he help at home?

A His grandparents **B** His father **C** His mother

3 Where does his father work?

A In a factory **B** In a supermarket **C** In a hospital

4 Who do Marquat's parents send money to?

A His sisters **B** His teacher **C** His grandparents

5 What does Marquat want to become when he's older?

A A journalist **B** A doctor **C** A teacher

6 Who's sitting next to Marquat on the first day of school?

A A small girl **B** A small boy **C** A tall boy

Grammar

2 Underline the correct word in the sentences.

Marquat is *fourteen* / *thirteen*.

1 School starts at a quarter *to nine* / *past nine*.

2 Marquat's parents *always* / *often* talk about money.

3 Marquat *never* / *sometimes* has problems learning things at school.

4 Marquat always sits at the *front* / *back* of the class.

5 Marquat *does* / *doesn't* do all his homework.

6 Marquat *talks* / *doesn't talk* to his classmates.

7 Marquat's *mum* / *dad* tells him he's special.

Speaking

3 Chapter 1 tells us about Marquat and his new school. Talk to a partner and answer these questions. How many of your answers are the same?

21st Century Skills

1 How did you feel on your first day at school?
2 Where do you like sitting in the classroom?
3 Do you talk to your classmates during lessons? Why? / Why not?
4 What subjects are you good at? Why?
5 What's the most difficult subject for you? Why?
6 Who's your favourite teacher? Why?
7 What would you like to do when you're older?

Before-reading Activities

Writing and Speaking

4 Who do you think says these lines? Choose between: *Marquat / Marquat's friend*. Discuss in pairs.

1 Everybody likes you. You're very popular.
____

2 I have to get good marks this year.
____

3 This is my country. My country is Britain.
____

Listening

3 **5 Listen to the next chapter. Check your answers in exercise 4.**

Chapter 2

A Good Friend

3

MARQUAT has only got one friend at school. His name is Alex. Marquat sits with him during the lunch break[1]. After school they sometimes walk home together because they live next door[2] to each other.

Marquat has one school friend, Alex. Alex is very popular but he isn't good at school.

Alex is very chatty[3] and fun to be with

'Everybody likes you, Alex! You're very popular,' Marquat tells him.

Alex smiles and looks at Marquat, 'Yes, but I'm not good at school.'

'Why not?' asks Marquat.

'I don't know. I don't think I study enough.' Then he says, 'You study a lot.'

[1] **lunch break** lunch time
[2] **next door** their houses are next to each other
[3] **chatty** talks a lot

Marquat doesn't say anything because he doesn't really know how much he studies. The only thing he knows is that he's never got enough time to study!

Marquat and Alex are very different. Marquat is really good at school. Alex's best subjects are PE and drama.

'You're very good at school,' Alex says to him. 'Nobody is as good as you in every subject!'

'But I like studying. I like discovering[1] new things about the world. It's very exciting! My problem is that I don't have enough time to study!'

It's true, Alex doesn't like studying very much. He likes listening to music and reading adventure stories. He thinks most school subjects are really boring: biology, French, physics and maths are his worst subjects! PE[2], music and drama[3] are his best ones.

This year is more difficult than last

[1] **discover** find something new
[2] **PE** physical education, gymnastics
[3] **drama** theatre studies and acting

year for Alex, 'I have to get good marks this year!' he says, 'My parents say I can go to watch the Manchester - Liverpool final in the Millenium Stadium.

But first, I have to study very hard.'

Alex wants to get good marks so he can go to the football final, so he must study hard. Marquat's parents never promise him things like that.

Marquat's parents don't promise[1] him things like that! In fact[2], they sometimes want him to study less! But for Alex, the football final is a good reason to study, 'The two best English teams playing against each other! It'll be so exciting!'

Alex and Marquat walk home together through Bute Park. Alex stops outside Marquat's house and looks at him. Alex is very sad.

Alex and Marquat are chatting about school. Alex isn't good at school like Marquat.

[1] **promise** say that you'll do something in the future
[2] **in fact** actually

Alex wants a different life from his parents, where he's free to travel and do what he wants. Marquat wants a different life too, but he doesn't want to travel.

'What's wrong?' asks Marquat.

'I've got the results[1] of my French test[2]. They're not good ...' replies[3] Alex. 'When I'm 18, I want to go to a faraway[4] world, to visit Africa or Australia. I want to work here and there[5] and travel as much as possible. I don't want to live like my parents: they do the same things every day! That's not my kind of life! What do you think, Marquat?'

'You're right, I don't want to live like my parents, either[6]. But I don't want to travel.'

'Don't you want to visit Nigeria, the country you come from, at least once in your life?' asks Alex.

'This is my country, Alex ... my country is Britain! Nigeria, Africa ... they're just names on a map for me,' replies Marquat.

[1] **results** final marks in an exam
[2] **test** class exam
[3] **reply** answer
[4] **faraway** (adj) very far from here
[5] **here and there** in one country and then another, free to move to another job when you want to
[6] **either** (here) also, too

'Oh!' says Alex, a little surprised, 'Don't you feel African at all[1]?'

'No, not at all!' Marquat replies firmly[2], 'Just because I'm black doesn't mean I'm not British.

I'm British, just like you!'

Marquat is angry and Alex is sorry for upsetting[3] his friend, so he changes the subject[4]. 'What do you want to do when you're older, then?' asks Alex, smiling.

'I want to do something I like, I don't want to do the same job my parents do. They only work to make money: I want to do a job I like.'

Marquat says he doesn't feel African at all and he wouldn't like to visit Nigeria. He says he's British like Alex. He's angry with Alex for what he said.

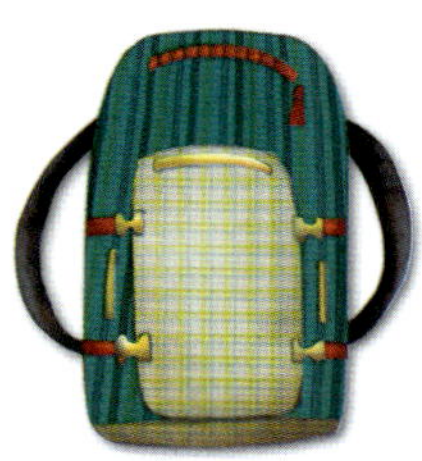

[1] **at all** in any way, just a little
[2] **firmly** (here) strongly
[3] **upset** make somebody angry and sad
[4] **change the subject** talk about something different

Alex is sorry that Marquat is angry so he talks about something else. Marquat says he wants to do a job he likes, not like his parents, who only work to make money.

'I'm sure you can do that, Marquat. After school you can go to university and then get a really good job!'

Marquat is angry with Alex because Alex asks him if he'd like to visit Nigeria. Marquat says Britain is his country.

Think

Why do you think Marquat got so angry with Alex?

Speaking

1 Answer the questions. Discuss in pairs.

How many friends does Marquat have?
He has one.

1 Where does Alex live?

____

2 What's Alex like?

____

3 Does Marquat have a lot of time to study?

____

4 What subjects is Alex good at?

____

Reading

2 Complete the two parts of sentences.

Alex and Marquat
- **A** ☐ cycle home together.
- **B** ☑ walk home together.
- **C** ☐ get a bus home together.

1 Alex enjoys
- **A** ☐ playing tennis.
- **B** ☐ listening to music.
- **C** ☐ playing video games.

2 Alex wants to get good marks so
- **A** ☐ he can go to a football match.
- **B** ☐ he can visit London.
- **C** ☐ his parents will be happy.

3 Marquat feels
- **A** ☐ African.
- **B** ☐ African and British.
- **C** ☐ British.

4 Marquat wants to
- **A** ☐ travel.
- **B** ☐ earn a lot of money.
- **C** ☐ have an interesting job.

Speaking and Writing

21st Century Skills

3 **Chapter 2 talks about Marquat and his friend Alex. Answer these questions with a partner, then write your answers. Do you agree about everything?**

1 Marquat and Alex are very different but they're friends. Are your friends the same as you or different?

2 Marquat has only one friend. Do you think it's better to have one best friend or lots of friends?

3 How do you choose your friends, or do they choose you?

4 What do you do with your friends?

5 Marquat gets angry with Alex about Nigeria. When do you get angry with your friends?

6 Do you talk to your friends if you have a problem? Why? / Why not?

Before-reading Activity

Listening

▶ 4 **4** **Listen to the start of Chapter 3 and choose the correct answer.**

Marquat's life is _difficult_ .

A difficult	**B** easy	**C** fun

1 His parents leave home at ________ .

A 7 a.m.	**B** 6.15 a.m.	**C** 6 a.m.

2 Marquat helps his sisters to ________ .

A make breakfast	**B** get dressed	**C** get up

3 Marquat's lessons start at ________ .

A 9.30 a.m.	**B** 9.15 a.m.	**C** 9 a.m.

4 At 11 o'clock there is a break for ________ minutes.

A fifty	**B** fifteen	**C** five minutes

5 Marquat always has lunch with ________ .

A his sisters	**B** his friend	**C** his parents

Chapter 3

Alex's Birthday

4

MARQUAT'S life isn't easy at all! His mum and dad leave the house at six o'clock in the morning and he has to get up at quarter past six. He makes his sisters' breakfast and helps them to get washed and dressed. He takes them to school at nine o'clock. Marquat has to be at his school at quarter past nine when assembly[1] begins, but his lessons start at half past nine.

Marquat has to do a lot of things every morning before going to school and he has lunch at school with Alex.

He has a fifteen-minute break at eleven o'clock and then an hour for lunch, between quarter to one and quarter to two. He always has lunch in the school canteen[2] with Alex.

[1] **assembly** a school meeting with all the teachers and students
[2] **canteen** the school 'restaurant'

A Faraway World

School finishes at half past three and then he goes to pick up[1] his sisters. Their schools are next door to each other in St Mary Street. He takes his sisters home and plays with them from four until five o'clock. He then studies for an hour. He makes dinner at six o'clock and finally sits down to eat with his family at seven o'clock.

After school he has lots to do too like looking after his sisters, studying and making dinner for his family, so he has very little time to see his friends.

He sometimes goes to work in his father's supermarket on Saturdays. On Sundays, he does his homework. This is why Marquat doesn't see his friends very often!

Alex's birthday is on 4th February and he's organising[2] a disco to celebrate[3],

[1] **pick up** collect, go and get
[2] **organise** prepare everything
[3] **celebrate** do something special on an important day for you like your birthday

Alex is having a birthday party, a disco, and he says Marquat must come, even if Marquat doesn't like the idea because he's shy.

but Marquat doesn't want to go. He's very shy and he doesn't like the idea of going to a disco!

Alex knows this, but he wants his friend to come, 'Come on, Marquat! Don't be such a spoilsport[1]! Come and have some fun!' he says.

Marquat shakes his head[2], but Alex says firmly, 'Don't say no! You're coming and that's it[3]!'

Marquat sighs[4] and says, 'Yes, OK, OK! I'll come.'

The disco is on Saturday afternoon. It's in a small room, but there are lots of flashing[5] lights and the music is very

1 **spoilsport** (expression) a person who never wants to have fun, who doesn't like parties
2 **shake (your) head** move (your) head from left to right to say 'no'
3 **that's it** (expression) no more talking about it
4 **sigh** a long sound of air that you make with your mouth to show that you decide to do something even if you don't really want to
5 **flashing** a light that goes on and off very quickly

›

Marquat is helping his father in his supermarket. He sometimes has to help him on Saturdays.

4,00

Marquat can stay at the disco for two hours. There are lots of people there when he arrives and he can't find Alex.

loud. Marquat gets there[1] at five o'clock. His sisters are staying with a cousin and he has to pick them up at seven. He's got two hours to have some fun!

There are a lot of people, but it's very dark inside the disco and Marquat can't find Alex. His other classmates are there and there are also a lot of people that he doesn't know.

Marquat goes towards[2] the dance floor. Alex is there, dancing and singing the words to 'Halo' by Beyoncé. Alex sees his friend. He stops dancing and goes towards him. 'Marquat!' he screams[3],

[1] **get there** arrive (at the disco)
[2] **towards** up to something
[3] **scream** shout very loudly

'Hi! Come on, come and dance!'

'Happy Birthday!' Alex shouts Marquat, but Alex can't hear him.

In the meantime[1], two girls come up to Alex and one of them says something in Alex's ear.

Alex looks at Marquat, but listens to the girl.

He starts laughing. The girl laughs, too.

Marquat starts to feel uncomfortable[2], 'What are they saying?' he thinks to himself, 'Why are they laughing? Are they laughing at me?'

'Come and dance!' Alex screams again.

Alex tells Marquat to come on the dance floor. He's having fun and laughing with some girls.

[1] **in the meantime** at the same time
[2] **uncomfortable** (here) not happy

Marquat thinks maybe Alex and the girl are laughing at him and he's upset. He says he can't dance then someone says something really horrible to him.

'I can't dance!' Marquat screams back.

Suddenly[1], Marquat hears a voice[2] in his ear, 'All black boys[3] know how to dance ...'

Think

How do you think Marquat feels when he hears these horrible words?

What do you think he should do?

[1] **suddenly** if something happens suddenly, it's quick and you're surprised by it
[2] **voice** you use your voice to speak or sing
[3] **black boys** (here) a really horrible way to talk to or about someone

›

Everyone is happy and dancing at the party except Marquat. He thinks Alex and the girls are laughing at him.

Reading

1 Put what Marquat does every day in the correct order. Number the sentences from 2 to 11.

- **a** ☐ He has an hour for lunch.
- **b** ☐ He studies for an hour.
- **c** ☐ *1* He gets up.
- **d** ☐ He plays with his sisters for an hour.
- **e** ☐ He helps his sisters to get dressed.
- **f** ☐ He has dinner with his family.
- **g** ☐ His parents leave the house.
- **h** ☐ He starts his lessons.
- **i** ☐ He takes his sisters to school.
- **j** ☐ He finishes school.
- **l** ☐ He picks up his sisters.
- **m** ☐ He makes dinner.

Reading about A2 Key

2 Complete the text Chapter 3 with one word for each space.

Marquat *doesn't* have an easy life. One day, Alex invites (**1**) ______ to his birthday party. Alex (**2**) ______ organising a disco. Alex tells Marquat he has (**3**) ______ come. Marquat (**4**) ______ stay for two hours at the party. When Marquat arrives (**5**) ______ the party, he can't find Alex at first (**6**) ______ it's very dark inside and there are a lot of people.

Writing

21st Century Skills

3 In Chapter 3, Alex invites Marquat to his birthday party. Write your answers to these questions.

1 When's your birthday?
2 Do you prefer to celebrate your birthday with your friends or your family?
3 What do you usually do on your birthday?
4 Do you like going to parties? Why? / Why not?
5 What do you have to do to organise a party?
6 What presents did you get for your last birthday?
7 Are you good at choosing presents for other people?

Before-reading Activities

Speaking

4 Look at the picture in the next chapter on page 43 and answer the questions.

A Are the boys happy?
B What do you think Alex is saying?
C What do you think will happen next ?

Writing

5 Finish the sentences.

1 I think Marquat will ________________________.
2 I think Alex will ________________________.
3 I think it will be a/an ________________________ ending.

Chapter 4

A Serious[1] Problem

▶ 5

Four boys at the party are horrible to Marquat and call him 'black boy'.

MARQUAT turns round[2]: there are four boys in front of him, all older and bigger than him.

Nobody says *black boy* anymore. It's very racist[3] and patronising[4], too.

The boys stand in front of Marquat and look him straight in the eye.

One of them waves[5] at Alex, 'Hi, Alex! How's it going[6]?' he asks.

'Not bad ...' replies Alex.

'So, *black boy*, why aren't you dancing?' The other boys laugh.

[1] **serious** big, important
[2] **turn round** to move your body so that a person is no longer behind you, but you're now face to face
[3] **racist** (here) unfriendly and dangerous way of talking to people from other races (African, Indian, Chinese)
[4] **patronising** as if you're better than the person in front of you
[5] **wave** move (your) hand to say *hello* or *goodbye*
[6] **How's it going?** how are you?

Alex doesn't like the the way things are going now, 'OK, guys[1], that's enough[2]! Marquat, come and dance with me! I don't want any trouble[3]. This is my party!' he says firmly.

One of the bullies laughs, 'Let's get out of here[4]! Let's go to a real party!' he says to his friends.

Marquat now wants to go home, but Alex doesn't want him to go, 'Come on Marquat, come and dance!'

Alex tells the bullies to stop being horrible to Marquat. Then he tells Marquat to come and dance. Alex is good at dancing but Marquat doesn't move.

Marquat follows his friend onto the dance floor. Alex is a very good dancer. Marquat watches him and doesn't move.

'Come on, Marquat,' repeats Alex.

'Move your body … left, right, left … move your feet …'

[1] **guys** (slang) boys and girls, everybody
[2] **that's enough** stop it
[3] **trouble** problems
[4] **let's get out of here** (slang) let's go

Marquat can't dance and leaves the dance floor. Alex doesn't understand his friend. He follows him and says that Africans are usually good at dancing.

Marquat moves one foot. 'Look,' says Alex 'like this ... just follow the music, listen to the beat[1]!'

But Marquat can't follow the music, he can't hear the beat: basically[2], Marquat can't dance!

'An elephant can dance better than me,' he shouts and walks away from the dance floor.

Alex doesn't understand him. He's disappointed in[3] his friend, but he goes after him[4], 'Why can't you dance?' he asks him,

'Africans are usually very good at dancing!'

[1] **beat** the timing of the music
[2] **basically** (here) in other words
[3] **disappointed in** sad and angry with
[4] **go after him** follow someone

›

Alex tells the bullies to stop being horrible to Marquat.

Marquat is very angry with Alex and says he's like the others, who think he's African. He leaves the disco, but Alex follows him and the bullies follow them too.

Marquat is shocked[1]! He can't believe what Alex is saying, 'You ...', he starts 'so, you still think I'm African. You also think that Africans can only sing and dance! Well I can't, Alex, so sorry!' Marquat is now very angry with Alex.

He looks at Alex and says, 'You're the same as all the others ...'

He leaves the disco, but Alex goes after him again because he wants to talk to him.

The four racist bullies follow, too.

It's only 6 o'clock in the evening, but it's already dark. In February, it always gets dark early.

Marquat walks towards the bus stop, but Alex calls him: 'Marquat! Marquat! Stop!' he shouts.

[1] **shocked** very, very surprised in a bad way

Marquat can hear him, but he carries on[1] walking. He's angry and disappointed.

Alex catches up with him[2] and starts talking, 'I'm sorry, Marquat', he apologises[3], 'don't be upset!'

'Please, Marquat,' says Alex, 'I can be really stupid[4] sometimes ... I know. It's just that with the lights, the music, the girls, the noise ... I just don't think sometimes before opening my mouth[5]!, I know that's not right. I really don't want to upset you, Marquat.'

It's dark outside and Marquat walks towards the bus stop. Alex catches up with him and apologises for what he said.

[1] **carry on** not stop doing something
[2] **catch up with someone** get to where someone is
[3] **apologise** say sorry
[4] **stupid** not clever
[5] **before opening my mouth** (here) before speaking

Alex apologises again for what he said and the two boys are friends again.

Marquat understands what his friend is trying to say:

'OK, Alex', he says. 'I understand.'

'Friends?' smiles Alex and puts his hand out.

Marquat smiles too, and shakes his friend's hand[1]: 'Friends!' he replies.

Think

What do you do if you say something that upsets your friend?

[1] **shake hands** look at the picture on page 47. Marquat and Alex are shaking hands

›

Marquat and Alex are shaking hands. They're friends again.

Reading A2 Key

1 Read about Chapter 4 and choose the best word (A, B or C) for each space.

Marquat turns around and there are four boys ___*in*___ front of him. They're all (**1**) ___________ than him. Alex doesn't want (**2**) ___________ trouble at the party so he tells Marquat to come and dance. Alex walks back to the dance floor (**3**) ___________ starts dancing. Marquat leaves the party and Alex runs after to Marquat because he wants to talk to (**4**) ___________ . He (**5**) ___________ want upset Marquat.

	A	on	~~**B**~~	in	**C**	at
1	**A**	old	**B**	oldest	**C**	older
2	**A**	any	**B**	a	**C**	some
3	**A**	but	**B**	and	**C**	so
4	**A**	he	**B**	him	**C**	his
5	**A**	doesn't	**B**	isn't	**C**	not

Speaking

21st Century Skills

2 In Chapter 4, some bullies say horrible things to Marquat. Talk to a partner and answer these questions.

1 Have you ever been worried about bullies?
2 What does 'cyberbullying' mean?
3 Do you know anyone who has had problems with cyberbullying?
4 If you have a problem with bullies, what should you do?
5 Why do you think people become bullies?
6 What do you do if you see a bully being horrible to someone? Why?

Reading

3 Match the two halves of the sentences.

	[f] Alex is		a	understand him.
1	[ ] Marquat doesn't		b	disappointed in Alex.
2	[ ] Marquat is		c	know how to dance.
3	[ ] Alex doesn't		d	follow Alex and Marquat.
4	[ ] The four bullies		e	decide to be friends again.
5	[ ] Alex and Marquat		~~f~~	a very good dancer.

Writing

4 Write a summary of the story so far.

____

____

____

____

____

____

____

____

____

____

____

Before-reading Activity

Speaking and Listening

6 **5 Tick (✓) what you think is going to happen in the next chapter. Discuss in pairs.**

1 Marquat fights the bullies. [ ]
2 Marquat breaks an arm. [ ]
3 The police come. [ ]
4 Alex and Marquat become friends with the bullies. [ ]
5 Life at school doesn't change for Marquat. [ ]

Chapter 5

Bullies

▶ 6

The four racist bullies call Marquat 'black boy' again. Marquat wants to run away but they stop him.

SUDDENLY, the four bullies are in front of them again.

'So, black boy' shouts one of them, nastily[1], 'why don't you learn to dance?'

'Why do they keep saying that!' Marquat thinks angrily[2] to himself and turns round. The four racist bullies are in front of him, laughing and pointing at him.

Marquat wants to run, but they stop him.

'We'll teach you a lesson[3], little black boy!' they say aggressively[4]. 'Except that[5] it's not going to be a dance lesson!'

Then Alex steps in[6], 'Look guys, just drop it[7]. Let him go ... he's a friend.'

[1] **nastily** in a bad and horrible way
[2] **angrily** in an angry way
[3] **we'll teach you a lesson** (idiom) you say this when you want to hurt somebody
[4] **aggressively** in a way that makes you afraid
[5] **except that** (here) but
[6] **step in** (here) say something
[7] **just drop it** (idiom) stop it

'A friend?' laughs one of the bullies. 'How can this little black boy be your friend?'

'Get lost[1], Alex' shouts another. But Alex doesn't move.

Marquat looks at the boys: there are four of them and they're too big for him and Alex to take on alone[2].

Marquat tells Alex to run away. The four bullies are bigger than him but he's not scared.

'Alex, just go, please ...' says Marquat.

Alex doesn't really know what to do, but in the end he decides to run.

Marquat now finds himself alone on the dark road. He doesn't know why, but he's not scared[3].

The bullies keep on saying things to him, 'Hey, black boy! Why don't you go home, go back to Africa!' they sneer[4].

Suddenly, one of the boys pushes Marquat. Marquat falls to the ground[5].

1 **get lost** (idiom) go away
2 **take on alone** fight against by themselves
3 **scared** afraid
4 **sneer** laugh nastily
5 **fall to the ground** fall down

The bullies push Marquat and he falls to the ground. Then Alex and others from his class arrive to help him and the bullies run away.

One of the others kicks him. Marquat gets up and manages[1] to hit one of the boys, but they're faster and stronger and Marquat falls to the ground again.

Suddenly, there are footsteps[2] and people start to arrive. Marquat sees Alex first, then he sees other boys and girls from his class running towards him: 'Leave him alone'! they all shout together. The bullies suddenly stop and run away. Marquat is still on the ground. Alex helps him to get up.

'Are you OK?' he asks his friend.

'Yeah[3], I'm fine', answers Marquat, looking at everyone.

'Thanks very much, guys!'

'That's what friends are for[4] ...' says Alex, patting[5] his friend on the back. Then he says:

›

The bullies push Marquat to the ground and Alex runs away to get help.

1 **manage** be able to
2 **footsteps** the noise you make when you walk
3 **yeah** (slang) yes
4 **that's what friends are for** (expression) friends are there to help you when you have a problem
5 **pat** hit but in a soft way

Things are much better at school now for Marquat. He and his classmates understand each other and are good friends.

'Marquat, I think you've got some blood[1] on your face.'

'It's nothing to worry about,' Marquat reassures[2] him. The bus arrives while they're talking.

Marquat looks at the time: it's quarter to seven!

'I have to go, I'm late', he says.

'See you tomorrow.'

He gets on the bus and goes to pick up his sisters.

Marquat's life at the new school is now very different: he respects[3] his friends and they respect him. He understands why his friends are sometimes confused about his nationality and his friends understand that Marquat is British, except that his parents are Nigerian. In the end, everybody agrees that friendship is what it's all about[4]!

Think

The bullies run away when they see Marquat's friends. What does that tell you about bullies?

[1] **blood**

[2] **reassure** say something so that a person doesn't worry

[3] **respect** when you like someone for what they are and don't laugh at them

[4] **friendship is what it's all about** being friends is the most important thing

The bullies run away when Alex and Marquat's other classmates arrive to help him.

Reading A2 Key

1 Choose the correct answer for each question about Chapter 5.

Where does Marquat meet the bullies again?

- **A** On the bus.
- **B** In the street.
- **C** In the supermarket.

1 What does Alex do?

- **A** He hits one of the bullies.
- **B** He runs to Marquat's home.
- **C** He runs to call his friends.

2 What does Marquat do to one of the bullies?

- **A** He kicks him.
- **B** He pushes him.
- **C** He hits him.

3 Who arrives to help Marquat?

- **A** Alex and his classmates.
- **B** Alex and their teacher.
- **C** Alex and Marquat's parents.

4 What do the bullies do?

- **A** They start shouting.
- **B** They hit Alex.
- **C** They run away.

5 What's Marquat's life at school like now?

- **A** The same as before.
- **B** Better than before.
- **C** Worse than before.

Grammar

2 Complete the sentences with the words below.

decide gets on respect ~~laugh~~ has is

The bullies *laugh* and point at Marquat.

1 Marquat ____________ alone on a dark road.
2 Marquat ____________ some blood on his face.
3 Marquat ____________ the bus to pick up his sisters.
4 Marquat and his friends ____________ each other.
5 They ____________ that friendship is the most important thing.

Speaking and Writing

21st Century Skills

3 Talk to a partner and answer these questions about the book. Then, write your answers.

1 Did you like the story? Why? / Why not?
2 Which was the most interesting chapter? Why?
3 Which character did you like best in the story? Why?
4 What do you think is difficult about starting a new school?
5 How can you help new students in your class?

Writing

4 Write a dialogue between Alex an Marquat one day after school.

____

____

____

____

____

Focus on...

Wales

Wales is on a peninsula in central west Great Britain. To the east, there's England, while on all the other sides, there's the sea. 3.15 million people live in Wales and the majority of them live in South Wales, in the industrialised cities such as Cardiff and Swansea. In central and north Wales, there are a lot of mountains.

Do you speak Welsh?

Wales has two official languages - English and Welsh. Welsh is a Celtic language like Cornish (spoken in Cornwall, in south-west England) and Breton (spoken in Brittany, in north-west France). Since 2000, all pupils in Welsh schools must study the language at school, even if fewer than a quarter of Welsh people speak it as a first language. This is a very different picture from the 1800s and early 1900s when speaking Welsh at school wasn't allowed and pupils were often punished for not speaking English.

The land of coal

Wales was once the biggest coal port in the world and this brought a lot of people from many different countries to Wales to live and work. These new people didn't know Welsh, so, even if more people lived in Wales, fewer and fewer spoke the Welsh language. However, as the coal industry became less important in the first half of the 20th century, many people lost their jobs and left Wales to find work in other countries such as the USA, England, Canada and Australia. There are also a lot of people who came from Wales in Patagonia, Argentina.

The land of song

Wales is known as the 'land of song' and has a large number of male voice choirs[1], which were born in the coal mines and ironworks of Wales. Every year in Wales, there are many festivals called 'eisteddfod'. The most famous is the 'National Eisteddfod of Wales' which is a festival of literature, music and theatre all in Welsh. It lasts eight days and every year it's in a different place.

Cardiff

- It's the capital city of Wales and also the biggest city with the most people in Wales.
- Bute Park is a big park. Here, you can find Cardiff Castle.
- The Millenium Stadium is the biggest covered stadium in the UK. It's used for matches and concerts and can hold 74,500 people.

[1] **choir** a group of singers

Focus on...

Immigration in Britain

In England the largest ethnic minority group are Southern Asians who can be found in the big industrial cities. A large number of Southern Asians (Indians, Pakistanis, Bangladeshi) arrived in Britain after their countries became independent from the UK in 1947. They started doing jobs such as driving buses and working in factories, but then began to open shops and manage post-offices.

Do you like Indian food?

Nowadays, the biggest influence of Asian culture in Britain is Indian food. There are about 10,000 Asian restaurants and it's probably the most popular food in the UK. Typical ingredients[1] in Indian cooking are curry, rice, various spices[2] and pulses[3]. Curry dishes can go from mild to very, very hot. However, the most popular dish of all in the UK is 'Chicken tikka masala', a creamy dish consisting of pieces of chicken, yoghurt and spices.

Music and films

Asians have also had a big influence on the music industry and Bhangra music (traditional Asian music) has become popular with young people, and many non-Asian singers and bands have used some of these influences in their own music. The daily lives of the Asian community can be seen in films like 'East is East' and 'Bend it like Beckham', which show the problems of growing up in Britain as a second-generation immigrant.

The new generation

Often the parents are very traditional and don't want to lose their own culture, while the children who were born in the UK, want to follow Western ideas. Sometimes parents don't agree with their children about their way of thinking, so they need to talk together and try to understand each other.
Many Asians have become famous in Britain for sport, music, films, tv and also in business.

[1] **ingredients** the things you use to make something to eat
[2] **spice** something you put in food, like pepper
[3] **pulses** dried beans and lentils are examples of pulses

Test Yourself

1 Read this information about the story. There are nine mistakes in the text. Find them and correct the information.

Marquat is 20 years old. He lives with his family in Cardiff, in Scotland. His parents come from Nigeria, a country in Africa, but Marquat feels British because his home is here, in Britain. Before going to school, Marquat has to take his two little brothers to their schools. When Marquat has time, he works in his father's shoe shop. Marquat wants to study. When he finishes school, he wants to go to New York and then he wants to find a job as a teacher. Marquat's classmates don't talk to him very much. Marquat has only got one friend at school. His name is Philip. Marquat is very boring and he likes studying very much. He finds most school subjects really interesting.

	Marquat is 14 years old	5	____
1	____	6	____
2	____	7	____
3	____	8	____
4	____	9	____

2 Choose the best answer A, B or C for each question.

1 Why does Marquat think nobody likes him?
- A ☐ Because his skin is black.
- B ☐ Because he's very special.
- C ☐ Because he sits at the front in class.

2 Why does Marquat like studying?
- A ☐ Because he wants to work in a supermarket.
- B ☐ Because he likes discovering new things about the world.
- C ☐ Because he wants to find a job as a dancer.

3 What can Alex do if he gets good marks at school?
- A ☐ He can organise a birthday party.
- B ☐ He can go on holiday.
- C ☐ He can go to watch the Manchester Liverpool final.

4 Who does Marquat meet at the disco?
- A ☐ Four boys, older and bigger than him.
- B ☐ A girl who wants to dance with him.
- C ☐ Alex's mother.

3 Write a different ending for the story.

Syllabus

Topics
Family, friends and ourselves
Jobs and the world of work
School and education: including school subjects
Daily routine

Tenses
Present simple and continuous
Past simple and continuous
Present perfect with *just, already, yet, never, ever, for* and *since*
Future with *going to* and *will*

Verb forms
Imperatives, infinitives, gerunds
Present and past simple passive forms

Modals
Can, could
Should (advice)
Must, have to (obligation)

Clause types
Main and co-ordinate clauses
Subordinate clauses after: *sure, know, think, say, tell, if, when, where, because*
Subordinate clause with *if* (zero and first conditionals)

Teen ELi Readers

Stage 1

Maureen Simpson, *In Search of a Missing Friend*
Charles Dickens, *Oliver Twist*
Geoffrey Chaucer, *The Canterbury Tales*
Janet Borsbey & Ruth Swan, *The Boat Race Mystery*
Lucy Maud Montgomery, *Anne of Green Gables*
Mark Twain, *A Connecticut Yankee in King Arthur's Court*
Mark Twain, *The Adventures of Huckleberry Finn*
Angela Tomkinson, *Great Friends!*
Edith Nesbit, *The Railway Children*
Eleanor H. Porter, *Pollyanna*
Anna Sewell, *Black Beauty*
Kenneth Grahame, *The Wind in the Willows*

Stage 2

Elizabeth Ferretti, *Dear Diary...*
Angela Tomkinson, *Loving London*
Mark Twain, *The Adventures of Tom Sawyer*
Mary Flagan, *The Egyptian Souvenir*
Maria Luisa Banfi, *A Faraway World*
Frances Hodgson Burnett, *The Secret Garden*
Robert Louis Stevenson, *Treasure Island*
Elizabeth Ferretti, *Adventure at Haydon Point*
William Shakespeare, *The Tempest*
Angela Tomkinson, *Enjoy New York*
Frances Hodgson Burnett, *Little Lord Fauntleroy*
Michael Lacey Freeman, *Egghead*
Michael Lacey Freeman, *Dot to Dot*
Silvana Sardi, *The Boy with the Red Balloon*
Silvana Sardi, *Scotland is Magic!*
Silvana Sardi, *Garpur: My Iceland*
Silvana Sardi, *Follow your Dreams*
Gabriele Rebagliati, *Naoko: My Japan*

Stage 3

Anna Claudia Ramos, *Expedition Brazil*
Charles Dickens, *David Copperfield*
Mary Flagan, *Val's Diary*
Maureen Simpson, *Destination Karminia*
Anonymous, *Robin Hood*
Jack London, *The Call of the Wild*
Louisa May Alcott, *Little Women*
Gordon Gamlin, *Allan: My Vancouver*

In this reader:

21st Century Skills	To encourage students to connect the story to the world they live in.
Key	A2 level activities.
Story Notes	A brief summary of the text.
Glossary	Explanation of difficult words.
Picture Caption	A brief explanation of the picture.
Audio	These icons indicate the parts of the story that are recorded. start stop
Think	To encourage students to develop their critical thinking skills.

The FSC® certification guarantees that the paper used in these publications comes from certified forests, promoting responsible forestry management worldwide.

FSC www.fsc.org MIX Paper from responsible sources FSC® C127663

For this series of ELI graded readers, we have planted 5000 new trees.

Book brief

1 Set in Cardiff, Wales, it tells the story of Marquat, a boy whose parents are from Nigeria.

2 Marquat feels British and gets angry when people say he's African.

3 School life is hard because Marquat is shy and his classmates don't have time for him, except his one and only friend, Alex.

4 The story touches serious issues like racism and bullying.

5 Its message is that through friendship and understanding, we can overcome all problems.